Go Whisper

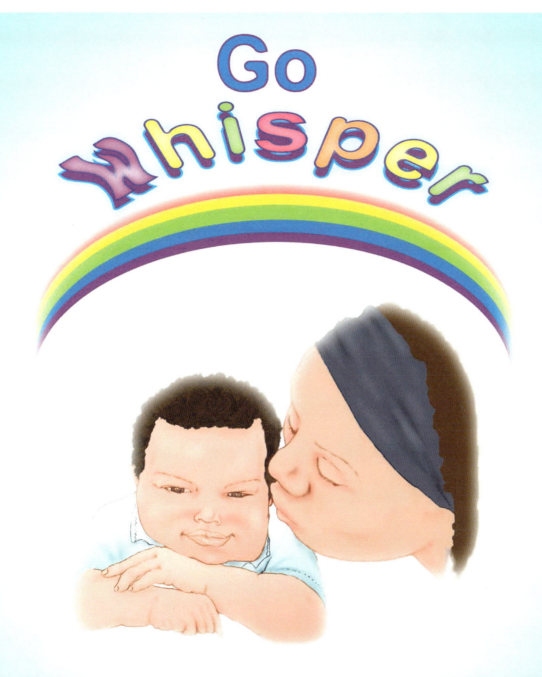

by
Fabian Howe

illustrated by
Joseph Funaro

ISBN 978-1477522653

Library of Congress Control Number: 2008904189

Published by Fabian Howe
Neptune, NJ 07754   USA
www.gowhisper.com

Illustrated by Joe Funaro

Printed in the United States of America

This book belongs to:

Daniel, Bruce, Davanni Canavan

Love, Joe, Lauren & Sweet Charlotte

We're so excited to share this book with you.
We know how important words are to our
success. You three have such bright futures
ahead of you. We can hardly wait to see
your accomplishments and how you'll change
the world! You can!!

Xmas 2013

Your tongue is the pen. Your words are ink. Your children are the paper. The words you write can not be erased.

- Fabian Howe

This book is dedicated to my two awesome kids, Ethan and Candace. They have shown me the meaning of unconditional love. They have taught me to intoxicate myself with the innocence of life, the joy of each day, and the pleasure of family. It is their tangible and intangible responses to *whispering* that has inspired this book.

Good morning, good morning it's time to rise.

We start our day with a loving word surprise.

We greet each other with a hug and smile.

We plug in our self-esteem and confidence file.

We embrace go whisper and make it our staple.

We extend love, believe and trust because we are able.

I love you. I appreciate you. I will always be here for you.

We discuss bullying others is not nice.

We praise others for their best, not for a price.

We cherish the friends we have near and far.

We go whisper with them even from afar.

I love you. I appreciate you. I will always be here for you.

We spend time reviewing homework after school.

We read several books because reading is cool.

We increase our knowledge by learning more.

We use go whisper to help us soar.

I love you. I appreciate you. I will always be here for you.

We play outside when the sun is up.

We ride our bikes and swing on stuff.

We go for walks and enjoy the day.

We encourage each other with the words we say.

We share good times and *go whisper* in the park.

We make the moments count with each remark.

I love you. I appreciate you. I will always be here for you.

We will giggle and laugh with each day.

We will always set aside time to play.

We share a love that is kind.

We *go whisper* with positive words in mind.

We say words like I Love You, how great that feels.

We build a foundation using go whisper as part of our ideals.

I love you. I appreciate you. I will always be here for you.

We build a consistent habit of using go whisper.

We empower one another with words and gesture.

We use words and actions to plant seeds that empower.

We accept and embrace change even if it's dour.

I love you. I appreciate you. I will always be here for you.

We celebrate our culture with food and dance.

We invite family and friends to celebrate in advance.

We enjoy movie nights and playing board games.

We discuss winning and losing and why they aren't the same.

I love you. I appreciate you. I will always be here for you.

We are blessed to have each other's love.

We exercise patience by rising above.

We understand trust and respect is a must.

We apologize and go whisper even after a fuss.

I love you. I appreciate you. I will always be here for you.

We cuddle, sing and read go whisper.

We make quality decisions that affect our future.

We give life to our words in the way we play.

We say what we mean and mean what we say.

I love you. I appreciate you. I will always be here for you.

We *go whisper* every day with harmony.

We have the most happy and united family.

We increase our confidence by taking action.

We say the words I love you, with great satisfaction.

I love you. I appreciate you. I will always be here for you.

We share a part of our day at the dinner table.

We give thanks for all we have because we are able.

We help clean up when dinner is done.

We go whisper about our day to share the fun.

I love you. I appreciate you. I will always be here for you.

We enjoy our family times together.

We build memories that get better and better.

We read *Go Whisper* each night before bed.

We build our self-image with words that are said.

I Love you. I appreciate you. I will always be here for you.

We raised our self-esteem on the extra mile.

We have fun with *go whisper* all the while.

We will have the best dreams tonight.

We will wake with a smile in the morning light.

Good night good night it's time for bed.

Sweet dreams sweet dreams as you rest your head.

I love you. I appreciate you. I will always be here for you.

THE START!

(personalize next page with your child)

_____(Child's name) **These are some of the reasons I Love You.**

1. _____

2. _____

3. _____

4. _____

5. _____

6. _____

I love you. I appreciate you. I will always be here for you.

To all Parents,

Children do not hear enough words that consistently relay the message we are blessed to have them. Parents today are very busy counting their days that we miss out on the opportunity to make our days count with our children. Like most parents, you probably rush home from work just to eat, sleep, wake up and do it all over again. Maybe you throw your children in front of the television just so you can have a minute to yourself; but unfortunately that minute usually lasts until it's time to put your children to bed. **Studies have shown that the lack of time spent with your children can negatively affects their self-image, self-confidence and self-esteem.**

This book was written to help you maximize the time you *do* spend with your children by engaging in the simple act of *go whispering* to them on a daily basis. *Go whispering* will boost their self-image, self-confidence and self-esteem. **Just five minutes a day spent *go whispering* to your children will have lasting results that will give them a head start in life.**

Why is this so important? How many times in a day do you think you say the word NO to your children? The odds are good that it's more times than you say YES. (Think about it the next time your children asks you for something.) The word NO is one of the smallest words in the dictionary but one that is highly overused. Its power can be devastating. **Fear of the word NO can be crippling to some and lead to a lesser life due to low self-esteem, lack of confidence and poor self-image.** For example, people would rather *die* than speak in-front of a group of people. That is easily attributed to a lack of confidence, poor self-image and low self-esteem.

Our children are the future; let's not cripple them. Let's empower them and raise a generation of children who are confident and have a strong sense of self. Let's call this generation . . .

GENERATION WHISPER.

Before we get started there is one ground rule. **Parents, you must stop speaking words of negativity to your children and, by all means, don't allow others to do so either.** Children learn by our example. If we use kind words, they will too.

Here is how *go whispering* started. My wife and I like to call this process, "Pray and Whisper" because we pray first and then we *go whisper*. We say to our children, "It's Pray and Whisper time" and Ethan (then 7, now 11) and Candace (then 3, now 7) will snuggle up with us, ears perked and ready to receive our kind and positive words. Since they were able to talk our children have asked us to pray and *go whisper* to them every night before they go to bed, and they still do.

In the previous pages I have written most of the things that my wife and I whisper to our children. I have also left additional space for you to **add your own ideas to personalize this experience for you and your children**. Maybe your kids have different abilities (academic or athletic) that you want to focus on or perhaps you can engage them by admiring other personal attributes (patience, kindness, empathy, sense of humor, respectfulness, etc.). Be creative and have fun!

Every morning, day or night, use what you have learned from reading Go Whisper and *go whisper* to your children. You will be making a conscious effort to put good things into the minds of your children; things you would be proud to hear them repeat. This is exactly why Go Whisper is so important. There will come a time when you will ask your children to *go whisper* to you, and when they do, it will astound you! You will not be able to hold back your tears of joy. My wife and I are still amazed by the *go whisperings* of our children.

It's never too late (or too early) to start *go whispering*; and it doesn't have to take place at home. **Go w*hispering* can happen at any place and at any time**. Make *go whispering* fun, surprise them sometimes by nibbling on their ears . . . ha-ha-ha!

Enjoy your Go Whisper journey and know that **the time you spend *go whispering* to your children is building a greater future for them**.

It's harder to change an adult than it is to train and nurture a child.

GO WHISPER

Log-on to www.gowhisper.com and share your testimony.

27813007R00021

Made in the USA
Lexington, KY
27 November 2013